Weekly Reader Books presents

DOLPHIN

By Robert A. Morris
Pictures by Mamoru Funai

A Science I CAN READ Book

Harper & Row, Publishers
New York, Evanston, San Francisco, London

To my wife, Sally

This book is a presentation of Weekly Reader Books.
Weekly Reader Books offers book clubs for children from
preschool through junior high school.

For further information write to:
Weekly Reader Books
1250 Fairwood Ave.
Columbus, Ohio 43216

It is morning.

The large sun comes up

in the sky.

The sea is calm.

TWEET! TWEET! TWEET!

These sounds

are made by dolphins.

They are excited.

They swim around

a large female dolphin.

She is going to have

a baby dolphin.

First, a small tail

comes out of her body.

Then suddenly

her baby is born.

It is three feet long.

The mother dolphin is

eight feet long.

Baby dolphins
are called calves.
Grown-up female dolphins
are called cows.
Grown-up male dolphins
are called bulls.
The new baby is a male.

Dolphins are mammals.

They must breathe air.

The new baby must breathe air soon,

or he will drown.

The mother dolphin

quickly swims under her baby.

She gently pushes him

up to the top of the water.

SWISH! SWISH!

The calf takes his first breath of air.

His nose is on top of his head.

It is called a blowhole.

Now the baby swims by himself.

He will breathe air

when he needs it.

11

The calf is hungry.

He swims close to his mother.

She turns on her side.

He gets warm milk

from her.

WHIRR. WHIRR. WHIRR.

The dolphins hear a new sound.

It is a ship.

The dolphins swim toward it.

The baby dolphin swims
next to his mother.

He is a fast swimmer.

The baby dolphin

moves his tail flukes

up and down.

The flukes push him

through the water.

16

The fin on top of his back

keeps him from rolling over.

His front fins

are called flippers.

The baby dolphin uses them

to swim up and down

and to turn right or left.

17

The mother and baby
swim faster and faster.
They race to the front
of the ship.
Then they stop swimming.
They ride on the waves
made by the ship.

Other dolphins join them.

They dive and jump

and play in the waves.

Their skin is smooth and bare.

It is easy for them

to swim through the water.

It is getting dark.

The dolphins swim away

from the ship.

It is time to rest.

The baby calls to his mother.

TWEET! TWEET! TWEET!

He is hungry

for his mother's milk.

The dolphins rest and breathe

on top of the water.

They will rest

for several hours.

The baby dolphin

closes his eyes.

It has been a long day.

The next morning

the mother dolphin is hungry.

She must find food.

Dolphins hunt together

in a group.

A group of dolphins

is called a pod.

The pods hunt for food
every day.
They eat fish, shrimp,
and small squid.
Today they find
a large school
of mackerel.

The mackerel swim away.

But the dolphins are faster.

Some of them swim

below the school of fish.

Some swim to the right,

and some to the left.

Now the mackerel

are all close together.

It is easy

for the dolphins

to catch them.

A wounded fish swims

near the baby dolphin.

The baby quickly grabs it.

But the fish is too large.

The baby cannot hold it

in his mouth.

The fish gets away.

CHURP! CHURP! CHURP!

This is the sound

of killer whales.

Killer whales are enemies

of dolphins.

They eat seals, large fish,

and dolphins.

SLAP! SLAP! SLAP!

A dolphin hits the water

with his tail.

That is the signal for danger.

The mother dolphin goes quickly

to her baby.

All the dolphins swim away.

They swim faster and faster.

But the killer whales

are coming closer

and closer.

The baby dolphin is tired.

Some of the bull dolphins

stay near

to protect him.

Then the killer whales

see the large school of mackerel.

They chase the mackerel instead.

The dolphins swim away.

They are safe.

Each day the calf

grows larger and larger.

He is now six months old.

He is over four feet long.

When he is two years old,

he will be

as big as his mother.

Sometimes the mother dolphin
leaves her calf
to dive for food.
While she is gone,
two other cows
watch the baby.
They help the mother dolphin
care for her calf.

The baby dolphin

cannot dive as deep

as his mother.

He can stay under water

for only three minutes.

The mother dolphin can dive

one hundred feet deep.

The deep water is cold.

But she has a thick layer of fat

under her skin.

The fat keeps her warm.

She stays under water

for six minutes.

The mother dolphin comes back
with a fish in her mouth.
She lets the fish go.
She wants the calf
to catch it by himself.

The calf chases the fish

and holds it with his teeth.

His small teeth are not like

baby teeth.

He will keep them

all of his life.

They will grow bigger

as he grows bigger.

The calf does not chew the fish.

He swallows it whole.

WHIRR. WHIRR. WHIRR.

A shrimp boat is coming.

Men pull in the large nets.

The nets are full of

shrimp and fish.

The men take the shrimp,

but they do not want the fish.

They throw them

back into the sea.

The dolphins swim up quickly

and eat the fish.

Sometimes the water is muddy.

The dolphins cannot see the fish.

CLICK! CLICK! CLICK!

The dolphins make

special sounds.

These sounds go through the water.

They hit the fish

and bounce back

to the dolphins.

These sounds

tell the dolphins

where the fish are.

CLICK! CLICK! CLICK!

The baby dolphin swims

back and forth

eating small fish.

Suddenly, there is a huge animal

in the muddy water.

It is much bigger than

the mother dolphin.

It is a giant tiger shark.

The shark is after the fish, too.

SLAP! SLAP! SLAP!

One of the dolphins

makes the danger sound.

It is too late!

The shark catches the baby dolphin

by the flipper.

The little dolphin

is wounded.

The tip of his flipper

is gone.

Many bull dolphins

swim toward the shark.

They hit the shark

with their beaks.

The shark is hurt.

He swims away.

The baby dolphin

needs air.

Two dolphins swim

under him.

They push him up

to the top of the water.

Now he can breathe.

The dolphin pod

stays near the baby

to protect him.

He is not hurt badly.

His flipper will soon heal.

TWEET! TWEET! TWEET!

The mother dolphin is calling.

The baby dolphin rushes

to her side.

It is time to get milk.

After he is one year old,

the dolphin calf

will not need milk.

He will be able

to care for himself.

61

The dolphin may live for thirty years.

He will stay with the pod

for a long time.

AUTHOR'S NOTE

This story is about a young bottlenosed dolphin. Its scientific name is *Tursiops truncatus*. Bottlenosed dolphins are found along the Atlantic coasts of the United States and Europe. In captivity they are easily trained and are very friendly toward people.